To

_____

From

_____

365 Smiles a Year For Dog Lovers

365 Smiles a Year For Dog Lovers
Copyright © 2006 by FaithPoint Press
Produced by Cliff Road Books

All rights reserved. No part of this book may be reproduced in any form or by any electronic or mechanical means, including information storage and retrieval systems, without written permission from the publisher.

Scripture taken from the HOLY BIBLE: NEW INTERNATIONAL VERSION®. NIV®. Copyright © 1973, 1978, 1984 by International Bible Society. Used by permission of The Zondervan Corporation.

The "NIV" and "New International Version" trademarks are registered in the United States Patent and Trademark Office by International Bible Society. All rights reserved.

ISBN-13: 978-1-58173-574-1
ISBN-10: 1-58173-574-X

Book design by Pat Covert

Printed in China

365 Smiles a Year For Dog Lovers

January 1

There is no psychiatrist in the world like a puppy licking your face.
Ben Williams

January 2

Being patted is what it is all about.
Roger A. Caras

January 3

Dogs are people, too.
Unknown

January 4

Dogs are us, only innocent.

Cynthia Heimel

January 5

Scratch a dog, and you'll find a permanent job.

Franklin P. Jones

January 6

None are as fiercely loyal as dog people. In return, no doubt, for the never-ending loyalty of dogs.

Linda Shrieves

January 7

Did you ever notice when you blow in a dog's face, he gets mad at you? But when you take him in a car, he sticks his head out the window.

Steve Bluestone

January 8

The Chow is a dog, who is a master, looking for a master, who is not a dog.

Unknown

January 9

In the world which we know, among the different and primitive geniuses that preside over the evolution of the several species, there exists not one, excepting that of the dog, that ever gave a thought to the presence of man.

Maurice Maeterlinck

January 10

The best way to get a puppy is to beg for a baby brother—and they'll settle for a puppy every time.

Winston Pendelton

January 11

Tell me, if you can, of anything that's finer than an evening in camp with a rare old friend and a dog after one's heart.

Nash Buckingham

January 12

The pug is living proof that God has a sense of humor.
Margo Kaufman

January 13

A Canadian psychologist is selling a video that teaches you how to test your dog's IQ. Here's how it works: If you spend $12.99 for the video, your dog is smarter than you.

Jay Leno

January 14

It is no coincidence that man's best friend cannot talk.

Unknown

January 15

If you don't own a dog, at least one, there is not necessarily anything wrong with you, but there may be something wrong with your life.

Roger A. Caras

January 16

To live long, eat like a cat,
drink like a dog.
German Proverb

January 17

A righteous man cares for the needs of his animal.

Proverbs 12:10a

January 18

Every dog must have his day.
Jonathan Swift

January 19

When a dog bites a man, that is not news, but when a man bites a dog, that is news.

Charles Anderson Dana

January 20

There is only one smartest dog in the world, and every boy has it.

Unknown

January 21

Poodles always listen attentively while being scolded—looking innocent, bewildered, and misunderstood.

James Thurber

January 22

Children and dogs are as necessary to the welfare of the country as Wall Street and the railroads.

Harry S. Truman

January 23

[Dogs] never talk about themselves but listen to you while you talk about yourself, and keep up an appearance of being interested in the conversation.

Jerome K. Jerome

January 24

The factory of the future will have only two employees, a man and a dog. The man will be there to feed the dog. The dog will be there to keep the man from touching the equipment.

Warren G. Bennis

January 25

Brothers and Sisters, I bid you beware of giving your heart to a dog to tear.

Rudyard Kipling

January 26

A dog with two homes is never any good.
Irish Proverb

January 27

When it's raining cats and dogs, be sure not to step in the poodles.

Unknown

January 28

One dog barks at something, the rest bark at him.

Chinese Proverb

January 29

Of all the things I miss from veterinary practice, puppy breath is one of the most fond memories!

Dr. Tom Cat

January 30

No animal should ever jump up on the dining-room furniture unless absolutely certain that he can hold his own in the conversation.

Fran Lebowitz

January 31

All in the town were still asleep, when the sun came up with a shout and leap. In the lonely streets unseen by man, a little dog danced. And the day began.

Rupert Brooke

February 1

His was the Collie heritage—the stark need for comradeship coupled with the unconscious craving to be owned by man and to give his devotion to man, his god.

Albert Payson Terhune

February 2

The great pleasure of a dog is that you may make a fool of yourself with him, and not only will he not scold you, but he will make a fool of himself, too.

Samuel Butler

February 3

A dog can express more with his tail in minutes than his owner can express with his tongue in hours.

Unknown

February 4

It is pretty hard to make the tail wag the dog.
Sidney Post Simpson

February 5

To his dog, every man is Napoleon; hence the constant popularity of dogs.
Aldous Huxley

February 6

No one appreciates the very special genius of your conversation as the dog does.

Christopher Morley

February 7

I can train any dog in five minutes. It's training the owner that takes longer.

Barbara Woodhouse

February 8

A dog without teeth will also attack a bone.
Yiddish Proverb

February 9

If your dog is too fat, you are not getting enough exercise.

Unknown

February 10

Dachshunds are ideal dogs for small children, as they are already stretched and pulled to such a length that the child cannot do much harm one way or the other.

Robert Benchley

February 11

We are alone, absolutely alone on this chance planet, and, amid all the forms of life that surround us, not one, excepting the dog, has made an alliance with us.

Maurice Maeterlinck

February 12

When an animal has feelings that are delicate and refined, and when they can be further perfected by education, then it becomes worthy of joining human society. To the highest degree the dog has all these qualities that merit human attention.

Count of Buffon

February 13

You ask of my companions. Hills, sir, and the sundown, and a dog as large as myself that my father bought me. They are better than human beings, because they know but do not tell.

Emily Dickinson

February 14

You can talk to a dog all day long, but he's just looking at you and thinking, "Where's the ball?"

Mike Myers

February 15

But ask the animals, and they will teach you, or the birds of the air, and they will tell you.

Job 12:7

February 16

I hope if dogs ever take over the world, and they choose a king, they don't just go by size, because I bet there are some Chihuahuas with some good ideas.

Jack Handy

February 17

My dog is half pit bull, half poodle. Not much of a watchdog, but a vicious gossip!

Craig Shoemaker

February 18

Every animal knows more than you do.
Native American Proverb

February 19

You think dogs will not be in heaven? I tell you, they will be there long before any of us.

Robert Louis Stevenson

February 20

Like many other much-loved humans, they believed that they owned their dogs, instead of realizing that their dogs owned them.

D. Smith

February 21

I talk to him when I'm lonesome; and I'm sure he understands. When he looks at me so attentively, and gently licks my hands; then he rubs his nose on my tailored clothes, but I never say naught. For . . . I can buy more clothes, but never a friend like that.

W. Dayton Wedgefarth

February 22

The idea that leisure is of value in itself is only conditionally true. The average man simply spends his leisure as a dog spends it. His recreations are all puerile, and the time supposed to benefit him really only stupefies him.

Unknown

February 23

The world was conquered through the understanding of dogs; the world exists through the understanding of dogs.

Friedrich Nietzche

February 24

Dogs love their friends and bite their enemies, quite unlike people, who are incapable of pure love and always have to mix love and hate in their object-relations.

Sigmund Freud

February 25

Happiness to a dog is what lies on the other side of a door.
Charleton Ogburn Jr.

February 26

God ... sat down for a moment when the dog was finished in order to watch it ... and to know that it was good, that nothing was lacking, that it could not have been made better.

Rainer Maria Rilke

February 27

Where did it come from, and at what moment in time did it walk out of the deserts and forest to sleep at the foot of man?

Mordecai Siegal

February 28

A man's dog stands by him in prosperity and poverty, in health and sickness. He will sleep on the cold ground where the wintry winds blow and the snow drives fiercely, if only he may be near his master's side.

George G. Vest

February 29

Generally, or at least very often, people with a deep interest in animals are the best people around.

Roger A. Caras

March 1

I know that dogs are pack animals, but it's difficult to imagine a pack of standard poodles, ... and if there was such a thing as a pack of standard poodles, where would they rove to? Bloomingdale's?

Yvonne Clifford

March 2

Ever consider what they must think of us? I mean, here we come back from a grocery store with the most amazing haul—chicken, pork, half cow. They must think we're the greatest hunters on earth!

Anne Tyler

March 3

From the dog's point of view, his master is an elongated and abnormally cunning dog.
Mabel Louise Robinson

March 4

When a dog barks at the moon, then it is religion, but when he barks at strangers, it is patriotism!

David Starr Jordan

March 5

If you are a dog and your owner suggests that you wear a sweater, . . . suggest that he wear a tail.

Fran Lebowitz

March 6

A piece of grass a day keeps the vet away.

Unknown

March 7

If a dog will not come to you after having looked you in the face, you should go home and examine your conscience.

Woodrow Wilson

March 8

Better to be a dog in times of peace
than a human being in
times of trouble.

Chinese Proverb

March 9

If animals could speak, the dog would be a blundering outspoken fellow, but the cat would have the rare grace of never saying a word too much.

Mark Twain

March 10

I wonder if other dogs think poodles are members of a weird religious cult.

Rita Rudner

March 11

You can say any foolish thing to a dog, and the dog will give you this look that says, "My God, you're right! I never would've thought of that!"

Dave Barry

March 12

A dog's warmth provides the friendliest blanket.

Unknown

March 13

It's funny how dogs and cats know the inside of folks better than other folks do, isn't it?

Eleanor H. Porter

March 14

I've seen a look in dogs' eyes, a quickly vanishing look of amazed contempt, and I am convinced that basically dogs think humans are nuts.

John Steinbeck

March 15

When a dog runs at you, whistle for him.
Henry David Thoreau

March 16

The only creatures that are evolved enough to convey pure love are dogs and infants.
Johnny Depp

March 17

Histories are more full of examples
of the fidelity of dogs
than of friends.

Alexander Pope

March 18

When a dog wags her tail and barks at the same time, how do you know which end to believe?

Unknown

March 19

The disposition of noble dogs is to be gentle with people they know and the opposite with those they don't know.... How, then, can the dog be anything other than a lover of learning since it defines what's its own and what's alien.

Plato

March 20

> 'Tis sweet to know there is an eye will mark our coming and look brighter when we come.
>
> **Lord Byron**

March 21

How many are your works, O Lord! In wisdom you made them all; the earth is full of your creatures.

Psalm 104:24

March 22

All knowledge, the totality of all questions and all answers, is contained in the dog.
Franz Kafka

March 23

Dogs are not our whole life, but they make our lives whole.

Roger A. Caras

March 24

If you want the best seat in the house, move the dog.

Unknown

March 25

My empty waterdish mocks me.
Bob the Dog

March 26

Let dogs delight to bark and bite, for God hath made them so.
Isaac Watts

March 27

Only mad dogs and Englishmen go out in the noonday sun.
Indian Proverb

March 28

If your dog thinks you're the greatest person in the world, don't seek a second opinion.
Jim Fiebig

March 29

Dogs love company. They place it first on their short list of needs.

J. R. Ackerley

March 30

A dog believes you are what you think you are.

Unknown

March 31

Dogs are miracles with paws.
Susan Ariel Rainbow Kennedy

April 1

Properly trained, a man can be dog's best friend.
Corey Ford

April 2

Did you ever walk into a room and forget why you walked in? I think that is how dogs spend their lives.

Sue Murphy

April 3

If more of us were like dogs, we'd be better off.
Jay Dickey

April 4

Dogs are very different from cats in that they can be images of human virtue. They are like us.

Iris Murdoch

April 5

In a perfect world, every dog would have a home, and every home would have a dog.

Unknown

April 6

No animal I know of can consistently be more of a friend and companion than a dog.

Stanley Leinwoll

April 7

Dogs feel very strongly that they should always go with you in the car, in case the need should arise for them to bark violently at nothing right in your ear.

Dave Barry

April 8

Dogs, the foremost snobs in creation, are quick to notice the difference between a well-clad and a disreputable stranger.
Albert Payson Terhune

April 9

The dog commends himself to our favor by affording to play to our propensity for mastery.

Thorstein Veblen

April 10

Fox-terriers are born with about four times as much original sin in them as other dogs.

Jerome K. Jerome

April 11

Everyone needs a dog to adore him, and a cat to bring him back to reality.

Unknown

April 12

Dogs remember faces, cats places.
English Proverb

April 13

I am not a cat man, but a dog man, and all felines can tell this at a glance—a sharp, vindictive glance.

James Thurber

April 14

Dogs laugh, but they laugh with their tails. What puts man in a higher state of evolution is that he has got his laugh on the right end.

Max Eastman

April 15

They say a reasonable amount o' fleas is good fer a dog—keeps him from broodin' over bein' a dog, mebbe.

Edward Westcott

April 16

What kind of life a dog ... acquires. I have sometimes tried to imagine by kneeling or lying full length on the ground and looking up. The world then becomes strangely incomplete; one sees little but legs.

E. V. Lucas

April 17

Dogs bark at milkmen, postmen, yourself, visitors to the house, and other dogs; some of them bark at nothing.... dogs tend not to bark at burglars, bailiffs, and income tax collectors, at whom they wag their tails in the most friendly manner.

Geoffrey Williams

April 18

Chasing your tail gets you nowhere
... 'cept back to where you started.
Unknown

April 19

Pomeranians speak only to Poodles, and Poodles speak only to God.

Charles Kuralt

April 20

The one absolutely unselfish friend that man can have in this selfish world … is his dog. … He will kiss the hand that has no food to offer; … lick the wounds and sores that come in encounter with the roughness of the world.

George G. Vest

April 21

Until you have bred dogs and have … painted them, it is difficult to realize that no two are identical in conformation. … It requires the intimacy of daily living with a dog to know … that his wet nose in your mouth tastes salty.

George Bird Evans

April 22

Politics are not my concern... they impressed me as a dog's life without a dog's decencies.

Rudyard Kipling

April 23

I am called a dog because I fawn on those who give me anything, I yelp at those who refuse, and I set my teeth in rascals.

Diogenes

April 24

Cats always land on their feet. Dogs won't even let you throw them.

Unknown

April 25

Those who sleep with dogs will rise with fleas.
Italian Proverb

April 26

Dogs … fight for honor at the first challenge, … and they do not for all their marvelous instincts appear to know about death. Being such wonderfully uncomplicated beings, they need us to do their worrying.

George Bird Evans

April 27

By and large, people who enjoy teaching animals to roll over will find themselves happier with a dog.

Barbara Holland

April 28

I have no dog, but it must be somewhere there's one belongs to me—a little chap with wagging tail, and dark brown eyes that never quail, but look you through, and through, and through, with love unspeakable and true.

John Kendrick Bangs

April 29

If you think dogs can't count, try putting three dog biscuits in your pocket and then giving Fido only two of them.

Phil Pastoret

April 30

Never trust a dog to watch your food.

Unknown

May 1

If dogs could talk, perhaps we would find it as hard to get along with them as we do with people.

Karel Capek

May 2

A door is what a dog is perpetually on the wrong side of.
Ogden Nash

May 3

A dog will flatter you, but you have to flatter the cat.
George Mikes

May 4

Labradors [are] lousy watchdogs. They usually bark when there is a stranger about, but it is an expression of unmitigated joy at the chance to meet somebody new, not a warning.

Norman Strung

May 5

He seemed neither old nor young. His strength lay in his eyes. They looked as old as the hills, and as young and as wild. I never tired looking into them.

John Muir

May 6

If your dog doesn't like someone, you probably shouldn't either.

Unknown

May 7

They say a dog is a man's best friend. That's if you are lucky enough to get one of those "friendly" dogs.

Jimmy Fallon

May 8

You may have a dog that won't sit up, roll over, or even cook breakfast, not because she's too stupid to learn how but because she's too smart to bother.

Rick Horowitz

May 9

Dachshund: A half-a-dog high and a half-a-dog long.

H. L. Mencken

May 10

Yesterday I was a dog. Today I'm a dog. Tomorrow I'll probably still be a dog. Sigh! There's so little hope for advancement.

Snoopy

May 11

Dog, n. A subsidiary Deity designed to catch the overflow and surplus of the world's worship. ... his master works for the means wherewith to purchase the idle wag of the Solomonic tail, seasoned with a look of tolerant recognition.

Ambrose Bierce

May 12

Dogs are better than children. Even my friends with children say that. As a dog friend of mine likes to say, children are for people who can't have dogs.

Unknown

May 13

A house without a dog or a cat is the house of a scoundrel.
Portuguese Proverb

May 14

If you eliminate smoking and gambling, you will be amazed to find that almost all an Englishman's pleasures can be, and mostly are, shared by his dog.

George Bernard Shaw

May 15

And God said, "Let the land produce living creatures according to their kinds: livestock, creatures that move along the ground, and wild animals, each according to its kind." And it was so.

Genesis 1:24

May 16

Old dogs, like old shoes, are comfortable. They might be a bit out of shape and a little worn around the edges, but they fit well.

Bonnie Wilcox

May 17

Not Carnegie, Vanderbilt, and Astor together could have raised money enough to buy a quarter share in my little dog.

Ernest Thompson Seton

May 18

Every boy should have two things: a dog, and a mother willing to let him have one.

Unknown

May 19

Never stand between a dog
and the hydrant.
John Peers

May 20

A dog wags its tail with its heart.
Martin Buxbaum

May 21

Show a dog a finger, and he wants the whole hand.
Yiddish Proverb

May 22

A well-trained dog will make no attempt to share your lunch. He will just make you feel so guilty that you cannot enjoy it.

Helen Thomson

May 23

[There exists] a sharp difference in the mental capacity of humans and canines. For example, a human who is given an intricate problem will spend all day trying to solve it, but a canine will have the sense to give up and do something else instead.

Corey Ford

May 24

One reason a dog is such a lovable creature is his tail wags instead of his tongue.

Unknown

May 25

A dog knows the places he is thrown food.
African Proverb

May 26

Blessed is the person who has earned the love of an old dog.

Sydney Jeanne Seward

May 27

Man is a dog's idea of what God should be.
Holbrook Jackson

May 28

With the exception of women, there is nothing on earth so agreeable or necessary to the comfort of man as the dog.

Edward Jesse

May 29

The dog is a gentleman; I hope to go to his heaven, not man's.
Mark Twain

May 30

Some days you're the dog; some days you're the hydrant.

Unknown

May 31

He who pelts every barking dog must pick up many stones.
German Proverb

June 1

When a man's best friend is his dog, that dog has a problem.

Edward Abbey

June 2

The question is not, Can they reason? Nor, Can they talk? But rather, Can they suffer?

Jeremy Bentham

June 3

Bulldogs are adorable, with faces like toads that have been sat on.
Colette

June 4

If skill could be gained by watching, every dog would become a butcher.
Turkish Proverb

June 5

I like pigs. Dogs look up to us. Cats look down on us. Pigs treat us as equals.

Winston Churchill

June 6

Researchers have discovered that dogs can comprehend a vocabulary of 2,000 words, whereas cats can only comprehend 25 to 50.

Unknown

June 7

In order to really enjoy a dog, one doesn't merely try to train him to be semi-human. The point of it is to open oneself to the possibility of becoming partly a dog.

Edward Hoagland

June 8

Near this spot are deposited the remains of one who possessed Beauty without Vanity, Strength without Insolence, Courage without Ferocity, and all the Virtues of Man, without his Vices.... to the Memory of Boatswain, a Dog.

Lord Byron

June 9

A man's soul can be judged by the way he treats his dog.

Charles Doran

June 10

Anybody who doesn't know what soap tastes like never washed a dog.

Franklin P. Jones

June 11

Since I have taken to sleeping under the bed, I have come to know tranquility I never imagined possible. You never really know when it might be cookie time. And that's what dogs have taught me.

Merrill Markoe

June 12

Cats are the ultimate narcissists. You can tell this by all the time they spend on personal grooming. Dogs aren't like this. A dog's idea of personal grooming is to roll in a dead fish.

James Gorman

June 13

Cat's motto: No matter what you've done wrong, always try to make it look like the dog did it.

Unknown

June 14

Bring out every kind of living creature that is with you—the birds, the animals, and all the creatures that move along the ground—so they can multiply on the earth and be fruitful and increase in number upon it.

Genesis 8:17

June 15

Dogs are getting bigger, according to a leading dog manufacturer.
Leo Rosten

June 16

A hungry dog hunts best.
Lee Trevino

June 17

I named my dog Stay so I can say, "Come here, Stay. Come here, Stay."

Steven Wright

June 18

Our dogs will love and admire the meanest of us, and feed our colossal vanity with their uncritical homage.

Agnes Replier

June 19

Thorns may hurt you, men desert you, sunlight turn to fog, but you're never friendless ever, if you have a dog.

Douglas Mallock

June 20

Every dog isn't a growler, and every growler isn't a dog.

Unknown

June 21

Dogs' lives are too short. Their only fault, really.

Agnes Sligh Turnbull

June 22

The dog was created specially for children. He is the god of frolic.

Henry Ward Beecher

June 23

When a shepherd goes to kill a wolf, and takes his dog along to see the sport, he should take care to avoid mistakes. The dog has certain relationships to the wolf the shepherd may have forgotten.

Robert M. Pirsig

June 24

In order to keep a true perspective of one's importance, everyone should have a dog that will worship him and a cat that will ignore him.

Dereke Bruce

June 25

By what right has the dog come to be regarded as a "noble" animal? The more brutal and cruel and unjust you are to him, the more your fawning and adoring slave he becomes.

Mark Twain

June 26

Recollect that the Almighty, who gave the dog to be companion of our pleasures and our toils, hath invested him with a nature noble and incapable of deceit.

Sir Walter Scott

June 27

Dogs are really people with short legs and fur coats.

Unknown

June 28

Even a dog knows the difference between being stumbled over and being kicked.

American Proverb

June 29

I like dogs better [than people]. They give you unconditional love. They either lick your face or bite you, but you always know where they're coming from. With people, you never know which ones will bite.

Greg Louganis

June 30

Dogs have given us their absolute all. We are the center of their universe. We are the focus of their love and faith and trust. They serve us in return for scraps. It is without a doubt the best deal man has ever made.

Roger A. Caras

July 1

Know yourself. Don't accept your dog's admiration as conclusive evidence that you are wonderful.

Ann Landers

July 2

Love me, love my dog.
St. Bernard

July 3

The slowest barker is the surest biter.

Unknown

July 4

If you are a host to your guest, be a host to his dog, also.

Russian Proverb

July 5

Acquiring a dog may be the only opportunity a human ever has to choose a relative.

Mordecai Siegal

July 6

I like a bit of mongrel myself, whether it's a man or a dog; they're the best for every day.

George Bernard Shaw

July 7

The dog is the only animal that has seen his god.
Unknown

July 8

A dog desires more affection than his dinner. Well, almost.

Charlotte Gray

July 9

> My little dog—a heartbeat at my feet.
>
> **Edith Wharton**

July 10

Dogs and children know who like them.

American Proverb

July 11

I would rather see the portrait of a dog that I know, than all the allegorical paintings they can show me in the world.
Samuel Johnson

July 12

Dogs are neither human nor British, but so long as you keep them under control, give them their exercise, feed them, pat them, you will find their wild emotions are amusing, and their characters interesting.

V. S. Pritchett

July 13

A watchdog is kept to guard your home, usually by sleeping where a burglar would awaken the household by falling over him.

Unknown

July 14

A dog, I will maintain, is a very tolerable judge of beauty, as appears from the fact that any liberally educated dog does, in a general way, prefer a woman to a man.

Frances Thompson

July 15

The dog has seldom been successful in pulling man up to its level of sagacity, but man has frequently dragged the dog down to his.

James Thurber

July 16

Your righteousness is like the mighty mountains, your justice like the great deep. O Lord, you preserve both man and beast.

Psalm 36:6

July 17

When you leave them in the morning, they stick their noses in the door crack and stand there like a portrait until you turn the key eight hours later.

Erma Bombeck

July 18

We long for an affection altogether ignorant of our faults. Heaven has accorded this to us in the uncritical canine attachment.

George Eliot

July 19

Pay attention to two-year olds and puppies. They know what's important.
Unknown

July 20

Our perfect companions never have fewer than four feet.

Colette

July 21

Dogs have not the power of comparing. A dog will take a small piece of meat as readily as a large, when both are before him.
Samuel Johnson

July 22

She had no particular breed in mind, no unusual requirements. Except the special sense of mutual recognition that tells dog and human they have both come to the right place.

Lloyd Alexander

July 23

Whoever said you can't buy happiness forgot little puppies.

Gene Hill

July 24

A dog is the only thing on earth that loves you more than he loves himself.

Josh Billings

July 25

A dog at play has the mind of a wise martial arts master, a mind capable of perfect focus.
Unknown

July 26

My husband and I are either going to buy a dog or have a child. We can't decide whether to ruin our carpet or ruin our lives.

Rita Rudner

July 27

A barking dog is often more useful than a sleeping lion.
Washington Irving

July 28

Let sleeping dogs lie.
Charles Dickens

July 29

You're only a dog, old fellow; a dog, and you've had your day; But never a friend of all my friends has been truer than you alway.

Julian Stearns Cutler

July 30

Personally, I would not give a fig for any man's religion whose horse, cat, and dog do not feel its benefits. Life in any form is our perpetual responsibility.

S. Parkes Cadman

July 31

When a dog is feeling down, all it needs is a little physical attention to make it feel happy again.

Unknown

August 1

Happiness is a warm puppy.
Charles Schulz

August 2

…when my old dog—completely exhausted after a hard day in the field—limps away from…the fire and comes over to [me] and puts her head in my lap…closes her eyes and goes back to sleep. I don't know what I've done to deserve that kind of friend.

Gene Hill

August 3

I think dogs are the most amazing creatures; they give unconditional love. For me they are the role model for being alive.

Gilda Radner

August 4

The censure of a dog is something no man can stand.

Christopher Morley

August 5

Hunger and ease is a dog's life.
Giovanni Torriano

August 6

It takes a strong-minded human to appreciate a string-minded dog!
Mary Webber

August 7

Never judge a dog's pedigree by the kind of books he does not chew.

Unknown

August 8

My dog is worried about the economy because Alpo is up to 99 cents a can. That's almost $7 in dog money.

Joe Weinstein

August 9

It is well to love a dog when you have the opportunity, for fear you should find nothing else worth loving.

Louise Honorine de Choiseul

August 10

I care not for a man's religion whose dog or cat is not the better for it.
Abraham Lincoln

August 11

A dog that intends to bite does not bear his teeth.

Turkish Proverb

August 12

Money will buy you a pretty good dog, but it won't buy the wag of his tail.

Henry Wheeler Shaw

August 13

To err is human, to forgive, canine.
Unknown

August 14

No man can be condemned for owning a dog. As long as he has a dog, he has a friend, and the poorer he gets, the better friend he has.

Will Rogers

August 15

Reverence, n. The spiritual attitude of a man to a god and a dog to a man.

Ambrose Bierce

August 16

I am I because my little dog knows me.
Gertrude Stein

August 17

A dog teaches a boy fidelity, perseverance, and to turn around three times before lying down.

Robert Benchley

August 18

If 'twere not for my cat and dog,
I think I could not live.
Ebenezer Elliott

August 19

Then God said to Noah...: "I now establish my covenant with you and with your descendants after you and with every living creature ... on earth."

Genesis 9:8-10

August 20

No matter how little money and how few possessions you own, having a dog makes you rich.

Louis Sabin

August 21

Dogs have more love than integrity. They've been true to us, yes, but they haven't been true to themselves.

Clarence Day

August 22

Try throwing a ball just once for a dog. It would be like eating only one peanut or potato chip. Try to ignore the importuning of a Golden Retriever who has brought you his tennis ball, the greatest treasure he possesses!

Roger A. Caras

August 23

The Airedale... an unrivaled mixture of brains, and clownish wit, the very ingredients one looks for in a spouse.
Chip Brown

August 24

People teach their dogs to sit—it's a trick. I've been sitting my whole life, and a dog has never looked at me as though he thought I was tricky.

Mitch Hedberg

August 25

The dog is a yes-animal, very popular with people who can't afford to keep a yes-man.

Robertson Davies

August 26

If there are no dogs in Heaven, then when I die, I want to go where they went.

Unknown

August 27

I wonder what goes through his mind when he sees us peeing in his water bowl.
Penny Ward Moser

August 28

It is scarcely possible to doubt that the love of man has become instinctive in the dog.

Charles Darwin

August 29

Dogs are our link to paradise. They don't know evil or jealousy or discontent. To sit with a dog on a hillside on a glorious afternoon is to be back in Eden, where doing nothing was not boring—it was peace.

Milan Kundera

August 30

You learn in this business: If you want a friend, get a dog.

Carl Icahn

August 31

Outside of a dog, a book is a man's best friend, and inside a dog, it's too dark to read.

Groucho Marx

September 1

You always sympathize with the underdog, except when the other dog is yours.

Unknown

September 2

What dogs?! These are my children, little people with fur who make my heart open a little wider.

Oprah Winfrey

September 3

When a dog wants to hang out the Do Not Disturb sign, as all of us do now and then, he is regarded as a traitor to his species.

Ramona C. Albert

September 4

What counts is not necessarily the size of the dog in the fight; it's the size of the fight in the dog.

Dwight D. Eisenhower

September 5

It often happens that a man is more humanely related to a cat or dog than to any human being.

Henry David Thoreau

September 6

The nose of the bulldog has been slanted backwards so that he can breathe without letting go.
Winston Churchill

September 7

Do not make the mistake of treating your dogs like humans, or they will treat you like dogs.

Martha Scott

September 8

A dog in desperation will leap over a wall.
Chinese Proverb

September 9

If you wish the dog to follow you, feed him.

Unknown

September 10

My dog! the difference between thee and me knows only our Creator.

Lamartine

September 11

A dog is like a liberal. He wants to please everybody. A cat really doesn't need to know that everybody loves him.

William Kuntsler

September 12

Speak soflty and own a big, mean Doberman.
Dave Miliman

September 13

An honest man is not the worse because a dog barks at him.

Danish Proverb

September 14

I like them all—pointers, setters, retrievers, spaniels—what have you. I've had good ones and bad of several kinds. Most of the bad ones were my fault, and most of the good ones would have been good under any circumstances.

Gene Hill

September 15

My dog, she looks at me sometimes with that look, and I think maybe deep down inside she must know exactly how I feel. But then maybe she just wants the food off my plate.

Unknown

September 16

If dogs could talk, it would take a lot of the fun out of owning one.
Andy Rooney

September 17

The small percentage of dogs that bite people is monumental proof that the dog is the most benign, forgiving creature on earth.

W. B. Koehler

September 18

If you pick up a starving dog and make him prosperous, he will not bite you. This is the principal difference between a man and a dog.

Mark Twain

September 19

"And to all the beasts of the earth and all the birds of the air and all the creatures that move on the ground—everything that has the breath of life in it—I give every green plant for food." And it was so.

Genesis 1:30

September 20

Man is troubled by what might be called the Dog Wish, a strange and involved compulsion to be as happy and carefree as a dog.

James Thurber

September 21

All trees have bark. All dogs bark.
Therefore, all dogs are trees.
Unknown

September 22

A dog is not "almost human," and I know of no greater insult to the canine race than to describe it as such.

John Holmes

September 23

Dogs need to sniff the ground; it's how they keep abreast of current events. The ground is a giant dog newspaper, containing all kinds of late-breaking news items, which, if they are especially urgent, are often continued in the next yard.

Dave Barry

September 24

If you get to thinking you're a person of some influence, try ordering somebody else's dog around.
Will Rogers

September 25

If you want loyalty–get a dog. If you want loyalty and attention–get a smart dog.

Grant Fairley

September 26

My dog is usually pleased with what I do, because she is not infected with the concept of what I "should" be doing.

Lonzo Idolswine

September 27

Without our dogs to walk, how empty our mornings, our evenings — our lives — would be.

Eric Rickstad

September 28

When some men go to the dogs, it is pretty tough on the dogs.

Unknown

September 29

Old age means realizing you will never own all the dogs you wanted to.

Joe Gores

September 30

There are three faithful friends: an old wife, an old dog, and ready money.

Benjamin Franklin

October 1

A bone to the dog is not charity. Charity is the bone shared with the dog, when you are just as hungry as the dog.
Jack London

October 2

A dog will quickly turn you into a fool, but who cares? Better your dog than your boss. I'm a fool for my dog and proud of it.

Unknown

October 3

Animals are such agreeable friends—
they ask no questions; they
pass no criticisms.

George Eliot

October 4

The greatest love is a mother's; then a dog's; then a sweetheart's.
Polish Proverb

October 5

It is fatal to let any dog know that he is funny, for he immediately loses his head and starts hamming it up.

P. G. Wodehouse

October 6

The best long-range shotgun load to have in one's boat for mallards is a fine retriever.

Nash Buckingham

October 7

There's facts about dogs, and then there's opinions about them. The dogs have the facts, and the humans have the opinions. If you want the facts about the dog, always get them straight from the dog. If you want opinions, get them from humans.

J. Allen Boone

October 8

Any member introducing a dog into the Society's premises shall be liable to a fine of one pound. Any animal leading a blind person shall be deemed to be a cat.

Oxford Union Society, London, Rule 46

October 9

I think animal testing is a terrible idea; they get all nervous and give the wrong answers.

Unknown

October 10

My dog can bark like a congressman, fetch like an aide, beg like a press secretary, and play dead like a receptionist when the phone rings.

Gerald B. H. Solomon

October 11

If I have any beliefs about immortality, it is that certain dogs I have known will go to heaven, and very, very few persons.

James Thurber

October 12

Better not take a dog on the space shuttle, because if he sticks his head out when you're coming home, his face might burn up.

Jack Handy

October 13

Heaven goes by favor. If it went by merit, you would stay out, and your dog would go in.

Mark Twain

October 14

> Lots of people have a rug, very few have a pug.
>
> **E. B. White**

October 15

The wild animals honor me, the jackals and the owls, because I provide water in the desert and streams in the wasteland, to give drink to my people, my chosen, the people I formed for myself that they may proclaim my praise.

Isaiah 43:20-21

October 16

First, you learn a new language, profanity, and second, you learn not to discipline your dogs when you're mad, and that's most of the time when you're training dogs.

Lou Schultz

October 17

The average dog is a nicer person than the average person.

Andy Rooney

October 18

Here, Gentleman, a dog teaches us a lesson in humanity.

Napoleon Bonaparte

October 19

Dogs live with man as courtiers 'round a monarch, steeped in the flattery of his notice... to push their favor in this world of pickings and caresses is, perhaps, the business of their lives.

Robert Louis Stevenson

October 20

The dog is a religious animal. In his savage state, he worships the moon and the lights that float upon the waters. These are his gods to whom he appeals at night with long-drawn howls.

Anatole France

October 21

The visionary chooses a cat; the man of concrete a dog. Hamlet must have kept a cat. Platonists, or cat lovers, include sailors, painters, poets, and pickpockets. Aristotelians, or dog lovers, include soldiers, football players, and burglars.

Unknown

October 22

I used to look at [my dog] Smokey and think, "If you were a little smarter, you could tell me what you were thinking," and he'd look at me like he was saying, "If you were a little smarter, I wouldn't have to."

Fred Jungclaus

October 23

I always like a dog, so long as he isn't spelled backward.

G. K. Chesterton

October 24

The most affectionate creature in the world is a wet dog.

Ambrose Bierce

October 25

The dog barks backward
without getting up.
I can remember when he was a pup.
Robert Frost

October 26

The dog wags his tail, not for you, but for your bread.

Portuguese Proverb

October 27

In a dog-eat-dog world, it is the dogmatic domain of dog lovers to offer dogdom a dog's chance to rise above the dog days for a doggone good time.

Unknown

October 28

There is no faith which has never yet been broken, except that of a truly faithful dog.
Konrad Lorenz

October 29

Say something idiotic and nobody but a dog politely wags its tail.
Virginia Graham

October 30

If a [person] be great, even his dog will wear a proud look.

Mohandas Gandhi

October 31

I love a dog. He does nothing for political reasons.
Will Rogers

November 1

The dog is man's best friend. He has a tail on one end. Up in front he has teeth. And four legs underneath.

Ogden Nash

November 2

A dog thinks, "Hey, these people I live with feed me, love me, provide me with a nice warm, dry house, pet me, and take good care of me.... they must be gods!" A cat thinks, "Hey, these people I live with... take good care of me.... I must be a god!"

Unknown

November 3

The fidelity of a dog is a precious gift demanding no less binding moral responsibilities than the friendship of a human being. The bond with a dog is as lasting as the ties of this earth can ever be.

Konrad Lorenz

November 4

Both humans and dogs love to play well into adulthood, and individuals from both species occasionally display evidence of having a conscience.

Jon Winokur

November 5

Rambunctious, rumbustious, delinquent dogs become angelic when sitting.

Dr. Ian Dunbar

November 6

The dog that licks ashes is not to be trusted with flour.
Italian Proverb

November 7

The more I know about men, the more I like dogs.

Gloria Allred

November 8

A man, a horse, and a dog are never weary of each other's company.

Unknown

November 9

The poor dog, in life the firmest friend, the first to welcome, foremost to defend.

Lord Byron

November 10

A dog is better than I am, for he has love and does not judge.
Xanthias

November 11

If a dog jumps in your lap, it is because he is fond of you, but if a cat does the same thing, it is because your lap is warmer.

Alfred North Whitehead

November 12

The dog represents all that is best in man.
Etienne Charlet

November 13

Beware of a silent dog
and still water.
Latin Proverb

November 14

The biggest dog has been a pup.

Joaquin Miller

November 15

A house is not a home without a dog.

Unknown

November 16

The King will reply, "I tell you the truth, whatever you did for one of the least of these brothers of mine, you did for me."

Matthew 25:40

November 17

Even the tiniest Poodle or Chihuahua is still a wolf at heart.

Dorothy Hinshaw Patent

November 18

I have always thought of a dog lover as a dog that was in love with another dog.
James Thurber

November 19

A really companionable and indispensable dog is an accident of nature. You can't get it by breeding for it, and you can't buy it with money. It just happens along.

E. B. White

November 20

He is your friend, your partner, your defender, your dog. You are his life, his love, his leader. He will be yours, faithful and true, to the last beat of his heart. You owe it to him to be worthy of such devotion.

Unknown

November 21

I am often surprised by the cleverness, and now and again by the stupidity of my dog, and I have similar experiences with mankind.

Arthur Schopenhauer

November 22

A good dog deserves a good bone.

American Proverb

November 23

You become responsible forever for what you have tamed.

Antoine de Saint-Exupery

November 24

I'd rather have an inch of a dog
than miles of pedigree.
Dana Burnet

November 25

If you want to be liked, get a dog.
Deborah Norville

November 26

If a dog's prayers were answered, bones would rain from the sky.

Unknown

November 27

The most reliable and intense dogs are the ones that achieve drive satisfaction by discovering success.

Sgt. Donn Yarnall

November 28

And many times I have thought that somewhere... there may be a special paradise for the good dogs, the poor dogs, the dirty and lonely dogs, to reward so much courage, so much patience and labour.

Baudelaire

November 29

To call him a dog hardly seems to do him justice, though inasmuch as he had four legs, a tail, and barked, I admit he was, to all outward appearances. But to those of us who knew him well, he was a perfect gentleman.

J. Kelly

November 30

Every dog should have a man of his own. There is nothing like a well-behaved person around the house to spread the blanket for him, or bring him his supper when he comes home man-tired at night.

Corey Ford

December 1

Among God's creatures, two, the dog and the guitar, have taken all the sizes and all the shapes, in order to not be separated from the man.

Andre Segovia

December 2

A dog has the soul of a philosopher.
Plato

December 3

A dog may bark, but his legs will never grow longer.
Unknown

December 4

Women and cats will do as they please, and men and dogs should relax and get used to the idea.

Robert A. Heinlein

December 5

If you don't want your dog to have bad breath, do what I do: Pour a little Lavoris in the toilet.

Jay Leno

December 6

When the Man waked up, he said, "What is Wild Dog doing here?" And the Woman said, "His name is not Wild Dog any more, but the First Friend, because he will be our friend for always and always and always."

Rudyard Kipling

December 7

The Dachshund's affectionate. He wants to wed with you: Lie down to sleep, and he's in bed with you. Sit in a chair, he's there. Depart, you break his heart.

E. B. White

December 8

The dog has an enviable mind; it remembers the nice things in life and quickly blots out the nasty.

Barbara Woodhouse

December 9

Work can wait another thirty minutes. There are more important things to do. Like throwing sticks.
Unknown

December 10

Now he has heard a whistle down the street; he trembles in a sort of ecstasy. Dances upon his eager, padding feet, straining himself to hear, to feel, to see, and rushes at a call to meet the one who in his tiny universe is sun.

Frances Rodman

December 11

A terrier does not revel in romantic solitude. Give her something noisy; and if a trifle low, so much the jollier.

Jerome K. Jerome

December 12

I once decided not to date a guy because he wasn't excited to meet my dog. I mean, this was like not wanting to meet my mother.

Bonnie Schacter

December 13

The dog has got more fun out of man than man has got out of the dog, for the clearly demonstrable reason that Man is the more laughable of the two animals.

James Thurber

December 14

If you can't decide between a shepherd, a setter, or a poodle, get them all—adopt a mutt!

ASPCA

December 15

Extraordinary creature! So close a friend, and yet so remote.

Thomas Mann

December 16

You call to a dog and a dog will break its neck to get to you. Dogs just want to please. Call to a cat and its attitude is, "What's in it for me?"

Lewis Grizzard

December 17

Until one has loved an animal, a part of one's soul remains unawakened.

Anatole France

December 18

One of the best feelings in the world is to come home to a puppy.

Unknown

December 19

Dogs are indeed the most affectionate and amiable animals of the whole brute creation.

Edmund Burke

December 20

An animal's eyes have the power to speak a great language.
Martin Buber

December 21

A dog's best friend is his illiteracy.
Ogden Nash

December 22

Dogs come when they are called. Cats take a message and get back to you.

Mary Bly

December 23

God, give me by Your grace what You give to dogs by nature.

Mechtilda of Magdeberg

December 24

My dog is not spoiled. . . . I'm just well trained!

Unknown

December 25

Puppies are nature's remedy for feeling unloved ... plus numerous other aliments of life.

Richard Allan Palm

December 26

It is just like man's vanity and impertinence to call an animal dumb because it is dumb to his dull perceptions.

Mark Twain

December 27

If you stop every time a dog barks,
your road will never end.

Saudi Arabian Proverb

December 28

A dog is a man's best friend.
A cat is a cat's best friend.
Robert J. Vogel

December 29

I am in favor of animal rights as well as human rights. That is the way of a whole human being.

Abraham Lincoln

December 30

My goal in life is to be as good of a person as my dog already thinks I am.

Unknown

December 31

The best thing about a man
is his dog.
French Proverb